Finding Peace in the Storm: Non-Resistance to Life's Challenges

Contents

Introduction

Non-resistance to life predicaments is a mind-set and approach to life that emphasizes acceptance and surrender to the circumstances we find ourselves in, rather than resisting or struggling against them. This philosophy recognizes that life is full of challenges, hardships, and difficulties, and that our resistance to these challenges often creates more suffering and stress than the challenges themselves. By embracing non-resistance, we learn to let go of our need for control and certainty, and instead cultivate a sense of openness, resilience, and adaptability. This approach can bring greater peace, happiness, and fulfilment to our lives, as we learn to navigate the ups and downs of life with greater ease and grace.

Chapter 1: Explanation of the concept of non-resistance

The idea of non-resistance proposes that one should refrain from fighting or rejecting what is occurring right now and should instead accept it for what it is.

It is often associated with spiritual and philosophical traditions that emphasize the importance of letting go of attachment to outcomes and surrendering to the flow of life.

In essence, non-resistance involves the acceptance of the present moment, whatever it may be, without judgment or resistance. This can be a powerful tool for reducing stress, anxiety, and other negative emotions, as it allows individuals to let go of the need to control or change things that are beyond their control.

Non-resistance can also be seen as a form of mindfulness, which involves being fully present in the moment and accepting things as they are, without judgment or attachment. By cultivating mindfulness and non-resistance, individuals can learn to live more fully in the present moment and experience greater inner peace and contentment.

It's important to note that non-resistance does not mean passivity or inaction in the face of injustice or harm. Rather, it involves a willingness to respond to challenges and difficulties in a way that is grounded in compassion and understanding, rather than anger or resistance.

Benefits of practicing non-resistance

Practicing non-resistance can have several benefits, including:

1. Reduced stress and anxiety: When we resist a situation or try to control it, we often feel stressed and anxious. Non-resistance helps us let go of our need for control and allows us to accept the situation as it is, reducing stress and anxiety.

2. Greater inner peace: Non-resistance helps us cultivate a sense of inner peace by accepting things as they are, rather than fighting against them. This allows us to be more present and, in the moment, rather than worrying about the past or future.

3. Improved relationships: Non-resistance can help improve our relationships by reducing conflict and allowing us to communicate more effectively. When we are not resisting or trying to control others, we can approach them with more openness and compassion.

4. Increased creativity and innovation: Non-resistance can help us approach problems and challenges with more creativity and innovation. When we are not stuck in a rigid mind-set, we can be more open to new ideas and solutions.

5. Greater spiritual growth: Non-resistance is often associated with spiritual growth and can help us connect with a deeper sense of purpose and meaning in life. By letting go of our need for control and accepting things as they are, we can cultivate a greater sense of peace and connection with the world around us.

How non-resistance differs from resignation or passivity

Non-resistance, resignation, and passivity are all terms that describe a lack of active opposition or resistance. However, there are important differences between them.

Non-resistance is a conscious choice not to resist a situation, person, or event. It involves letting go of resistance, but not necessarily giving up or accepting defeat. Instead, it is a way of acknowledging the reality of a situation and finding a way to work with it rather than against it. Non-resistance can involve finding a way to cooperate, negotiate, or adapt to a situation.

Resignation, on the other hand, is a feeling of acceptance or surrender to a situation without actively trying to change it. It can be a passive response to a difficult or challenging situation, in which a person may feel helpless or defeated. Resignation can be a form of giving up and may lead to feelings of despair or hopelessness.

Passivity is a state of inaction or lack of energy or initiative. It can be a response to a situation or event, but it is not necessarily a conscious choice. Passivity can be a result of feeling overwhelmed, apathetic, or discouraged. It can be a form of avoidance or procrastination, in which a person may delay acting or making decisions.

In summary, non-resistance involves a conscious choice to let go of resistance and find ways to work with a situation, while resignation and passivity involve a lack of active opposition or resistance but may not involve a conscious choice or an active response to the situation.

Chapter 2: Understanding Life's Challenges

The inevitability of challenges in life

Challenges are an inevitable part of life. No matter who you are or what your circumstances may be, at some point you will face difficulties, obstacles, and setbacks. Whether it's a health issue, a financial setback, a relationship problem, or some other type of challenge, these experiences can be difficult and even painful.

However, it's important to remember that challenges can also be opportunities for growth and learning. When we face difficulties, we are forced to confront our limitations, question our assumptions, and develop new strategies for coping and problem-solving. This can lead to personal growth, increased resilience, and a greater sense of self-awareness and purpose.

It's also important to recognize that challenges are a normal and natural part of the human experience. No one is immune to adversity, and everyone will face their own unique set of challenges throughout their lifetime. It's how we respond to these challenges that ultimately determines the course of our lives.

In summary, challenges are an inevitable part of life, but they can also be opportunities for growth and learning. By approaching challenges with a positive attitude, a willingness to learn, and a commitment to personal growth, we can navigate even the most difficult situations with grace and resilience.

Different types of life challenges (e.g., health, relationships, work)

There are a wide range of life challenges that people may face at different points in their lives. Some common types of challenges include:

1. Health challenges: These may include physical illnesses, injuries, mental health issues, chronic pain, and disabilities.

2. Relationship challenges: These may include difficulties with family members, friends, romantic partners, or colleagues, such as conflicts, communication breakdowns, or feelings of betrayal or abandonment.

3. Career challenges: These may include job loss, career changes, workplace stress, conflicts with colleagues or supervisors, or difficulties finding employment.

4. Financial challenges: These may include debt, job loss, unexpected expenses, or financial insecurity.

5. Personal growth challenges: These may include issues related to self-esteem, confidence, identity, purpose, and personal development.

6. Life transitions: These may include major life changes such as moving to a new city, starting a new job, getting married, having children, or dealing with the death of a loved one.

7. Spiritual challenges: These may include struggles with faith, loss of meaning or purpose, existential crises, or a sense of disconnection from oneself or others.

These are just a few examples of the types of life challenges that people may face. Each person's experience is unique, and the challenges they face may be influenced by a variety of factors, including their personal history, cultural background, and social context.

The role of adversity in personal growth and development

Adversity, or facing difficult challenges or hardships, can play a significant role in personal growth and development. In fact, many individuals who have overcome adversity report feeling stronger, more resilient, and more capable than they did before facing their challenges.

One reason for this is that adversity often forces individuals to confront their weaknesses and limitations, which can lead to personal growth and development. For example, someone who faces financial hardship may be forced to develop new skills or seek out new opportunities to overcome their situation.

Adversity can also foster a sense of resilience and determination in individuals. When someone faces a difficult challenge and can overcome it, they often gain a sense of self-efficacy and confidence that can help them tackle future challenges.

Moreover, facing and overcoming adversity can lead to greater empathy and understanding for others who may be facing similar challenges. This can lead to personal growth and development in terms of emotional intelligence and interpersonal skills.

However, it is important to note that not everyone responds to adversity in the same way. Some individuals may struggle to overcome their challenges and may experience negative consequences such as trauma or chronic stress. It is important to seek support and resources when facing adversity to promote positive personal growth and development.

Chapter 3: The Roots of Resistance

The roots of resistance can be traced back to the struggle of oppressed peoples throughout history. Resistance arises when individuals or groups feel that their rights or freedoms are being threatened or denied, and they take action to defend themselves and their communities.

Throughout history, there have been many examples of resistance movements, such as the American Civil Rights Movement, the Indian Independence Movement led by Mahatma Gandhi, and the anti-apartheid struggle in South Africa. These movements were all characterized by a determination to challenge unjust systems and fight for the rights of marginalized groups.

The roots of resistance are often found in the desire for social justice and equality, and in the recognition that change is necessary to achieve those goals. Whether it is through peaceful protest, civil disobedience, or armed struggle, resistance movements seek to challenge the status quo and create a more just and equitable society.

Today, resistance continues to take many forms, from the Black Lives Matter movement and the fight for immigrant rights, to the #MeToo movement and the global climate strikes. These movements remind us that the struggle for justice and equality is ongoing, and that individuals and communities can make a difference when they come together to resist oppression and demand change.

Why we resist difficult situations.

As humans, we often resist difficult situations because they can be uncomfortable or challenging. We are wired to seek pleasure and avoid pain, and difficult situations can be perceived as a source of pain or discomfort. Additionally, difficult situations can also trigger feelings of fear, anxiety, or uncertainty, which can make us feel vulnerable and exposed.

Furthermore, difficult situations often require us to step out of our comfort zones and confront our limitations, which can be uncomfortable and challenging for many people. It is natural to want to avoid situations that make us feel uncomfortable or challenge our sense of self-efficacy.

However, it is important to note that while resistance to difficult situations may be a natural response, it is not always the most effective or productive way to deal with them. Often, facing difficult situations head-on and learning to cope with discomfort and uncertainty can lead to personal growth and development. This can help build resilience, confidence, and a sense of mastery over challenging situations.

The impact of resistance on our well-being

How resistance can prolong and intensify our suffering

Resistance can prolong and intensify our suffering in a few ways.

Firstly, when we resist something, we often give it more power over us. For example, if we resist feeling sad or anxious, we may find that those feelings become even more intense and overwhelming. By resisting, we are essentially telling ourselves that the experience is too painful or difficult to face, which can amplify our emotional response.

Secondly, resistance can lead to rumination and negative self-talk. When we resist a situation or experience, we may spend a lot of time and energy dwelling on it and criticizing ourselves for not being able to handle it better. This can create a vicious cycle of negative thoughts and emotions that only serve to prolong our suffering.

Thirdly, resistance can prevent us from taking action to improve our situation. When we resist something, we may feel powerless and stuck, which can make it difficult to take positive steps towards change. This can further intensify our suffering and feelings of helplessness.

Overall, while resistance may seem like a natural response to difficult situations, it can make things worse by prolonging and intensifying our suffering. Instead, it is often more helpful to practice acceptance and self-compassion, and to take positive steps towards improving our situation where possible.

Chapter 4: Acceptance and Surrender

The power of acceptance in releasing resistance

The power of acceptance lies in its ability to help us release resistance and find peace in difficult or challenging situations. When we resist a situation or experience, we create tension and stress within ourselves, which can lead to feelings of frustration, anger, or anxiety. However, when we can accept a situation for what it is, we can let go of our resistance and find a sense of calm and inner peace.

Acceptance doesn't mean that we must like or condone a situation, but rather that we acknowledge it and recognize that it's a part of our reality. By accepting a situation, we can stop fighting against it and start focusing on what we can control or influence in our lives. This can lead to a greater sense of clarity and perspective and can help us make better decisions and take more effective action.

The power of acceptance is not just limited to difficult or challenging situations but can also be applied to our everyday lives. By accepting ourselves, our flaws, and our limitations, we can release the resistance we have towards ourselves and find more self-love and self-compassion.

Similarly, by accepting others for who they are, we can release the resistance and judgment we may have towards them and find more connection and understanding.

In summary, the power of acceptance lies in its ability to release resistance and help us find peace and clarity in difficult or challenging situations, as well as in our everyday lives.

How to cultivate a mind-set of surrender

Cultivating a mind-set of surrender can be a challenging process, but it is possible with consistent effort and practice. Here are some tips to help you develop a mind-set of surrender:

1. Acceptance: Start by accepting that you cannot control everything in life. There will always be things beyond your control, and the only thing you can control is your response to them. Accepting this fact can help you let go of the need to control everything.

2. Let go of resistance: Resistance to what is happening in your life can create stress and anxiety. Instead of resisting, try to surrender to the situation and embrace it as an opportunity to learn and grow.

3. Trust: Trust that everything happens for a reason and that the universe has a plan for you. Trust that even when things are difficult, it will ultimately lead you to where you need to be.

4. Practice mindfulness: Mindfulness is the practice of being present in the moment without judgment. By practicing mindfulness, you can learn to observe your thoughts and emotions without attaching to them, allowing you to let go of the need to control everything.

5. Practice gratitude: Gratitude can help shift your focus from what you don't have to what you do have. By focusing on the positives in your life, you can learn to appreciate what you have and let go of the need to control everything.

Remember that cultivating a mindset of surrender is a process, and it takes time and effort. Be patient with yourself and keep practicing.

The role of faith and trust in the surrender process

The surrender process often involves letting go of control and placing trust and faith in something bigger than oneself. This can be a spiritual or religious belief, or it can simply be a belief in the universe or the natural order of things.

Faith and trust play a crucial role in the surrender process because they help to alleviate fear and uncertainty. When we surrender, we are essentially acknowledging that we do not have all the answers and that we are willing to trust in something beyond ourselves to guide us.

Having faith and trust can also provide a sense of peace and comfort during difficult times. When we surrender to a higher power or to the universe, we can let go of our worries and anxieties and trust that everything will work out in the end.

However, it is important to note that faith and trust are not the same as blind obedience or resignation. Surrendering does not mean giving up on our goals or dreams, but rather it involves letting go of attachment to a specific outcome and being open to the possibility of different paths and opportunities.

Chapter 5: Mindfulness and Presence

How mindfulness can help us stay present and centred

Mindfulness is a state of being fully present and engaged in the current moment, without judgment or distraction. Practicing mindfulness can help us stay centred and focused, especially in moments of stress or chaos.

Here are some ways mindfulness can help us stay present and centred:

1. Increased awareness: Mindfulness helps us become more aware of our thoughts, emotions, and bodily sensations in the present moment. This increased awareness can help us recognize when our attention is wandering or when we are getting distracted by external stimuli.

2. Improved focus: Practicing mindfulness can improve our ability to concentrate and focus on the task at hand. By staying present and centred, we can better prioritize our goals and avoid getting overwhelmed by distractions.

3. Reduced stress: Mindfulness can help reduce stress and anxiety by allowing us to observe our thoughts and emotions without judgment. We can learn to accept our current circumstances and respond to them in a more calm and constructive way.

4. Enhanced well-being: By staying present and cantered, we can improve our overall well-being and quality of life. Mindfulness can help us develop a greater sense of self-awareness, self-compassion, and empathy for others.

Overall, practicing mindfulness can help us stay present and centred in the moment, which can lead to greater inner peace, clarity, and resilience in the face of challenges.

Techniques for cultivating mindfulness in daily life

Cultivating mindfulness can be a valuable tool for improving mental well-being, reducing stress, and increasing focus and productivity. Here are some techniques for incorporating mindfulness into daily life:

1. Pay attention to your breathing: Take a few minutes throughout the day to focus on your breath. Notice the sensation of air moving in and out of your body and try to keep your attention on your breath for a few minutes.

2. Practice mindful eating: Pay attention to the look, smell, taste, and texture of your food. Take your time to savour each bite and focus on the experience of eating without distractions.

3. Take mindful breaks: Take short breaks throughout the day to check in with yourself. Notice how you're feeling physically and emotionally and take a few deep breaths.

4. Practice mindfulness during routine activities: Use routine activities like washing dishes, showering, or brushing your teeth as an opportunity to practice mindfulness. Pay attention to the sensations, sounds, and sights of the activity.

5. Use mindfulness apps: There are several mindfulness apps available that can help you practice mindfulness in daily life, including Headspace, Calm, and Insight Timer.

6. Practice gratitude: Take time each day to reflect on things you're grateful for. This can help you cultivate a positive mind-set and increase feelings of well-being.

Remember that mindfulness is a skill that takes time and practice to develop. Start by incorporating small moments of mindfulness into your daily routine, and gradually build up to longer periods of mindfulness practice as you become more comfortable with the practice.

The connection between presence and non-resistance

The connection between presence and non-resistance can be understood through the practice of mindfulness. Presence means being fully aware and engaged in the present moment, without judgment or distraction. Non-resistance, on the other hand, means accepting the present moment as it is, without trying to change it or push it away.

When we practice mindfulness and cultivate a state of presence, we become more aware of our thoughts, emotions, and physical sensations.

We learn to observe them without judgment or attachment, allowing them to arise and pass away on their own. This helps us develop a sense of equanimity and non-reactivity, which in turn can lead to a greater sense of inner peace and well-being.

Non-resistance is a natural consequence of this state of presence and non-reactivity. When we are fully present and accepting of the present moment, we are less likely to resist it or try to change it. Instead, we learn to work with what is, rather than against it, which can lead to a greater sense of flow and ease in our lives.

In summary, presence and non-resistance are closely connected through the practice of mindfulness. By cultivating a state of presence, we can develop a greater sense of non-reactivity and acceptance, which can lead to a greater sense of peace and well-being in our lives.

Chapter 6: Compassion and Forgiveness

The role of compassion and forgiveness in non-resistance

Non-resistance is a philosophy or practice that encourages individuals to avoid resisting or fighting against negative or harmful situations or actions, and instead respond with peaceful, nonviolent actions. Compassion and forgiveness can play important roles in non-resistance.

Compassion is the ability to understand and empathize with the suffering of others. When we cultivate compassion, we develop a deeper understanding of the causes of conflict and suffering, and we become more motivated to find peaceful and nonviolent solutions to problems. Compassion can help us to respond to harmful situations with empathy and understanding, rather than with anger or aggression.

Forgiveness is the act of letting go of anger, resentment, and the desire for revenge towards those who have wronged us. When we forgive, we release ourselves from the emotional burden of anger and bitterness, and we open ourselves up to the possibility of healing and reconciliation. Forgiveness does not mean that we condone or approve of the harmful actions of others, but rather that we choose to move forward with a focus on peace and healing.

In the context of non-resistance, compassion and forgiveness can help us to respond to negative or harmful situations with a peaceful and nonviolent approach. By cultivating compassion, we can understand the root causes of conflict and suffering, and work towards finding peaceful and nonviolent solutions. By practicing forgiveness, we can release ourselves from the emotional burden of anger and bitterness and focus on creating a more peaceful and harmonious world.

How to cultivate compassion and forgiveness for us and others

Cultivating compassion and forgiveness for ourselves and others can be a challenging but rewarding process. Here are some steps you can take:

1. Practice mindfulness: Mindfulness is the practice of being present and aware of your thoughts and feelings without judgment. Regular

mindfulness meditation can help you cultivate compassion and forgiveness towards yourself and others by helping you recognize the emotions and patterns of thought that can prevent you from being forgiving and compassionate.

2. Develop empathy: Empathy is the ability to put yourself in someone else's shoes and understand their feelings and perspectives. Developing empathy can help you be more compassionate towards others, even if you disagree with them or they have hurt you in some way.

3. Practice self-compassion: Self-compassion is treating yourself with the same kindness and understanding that you would offer to a good friend. This means being gentle with yourself when you make mistakes or experience difficult emotions and acknowledging that everyone makes mistakes and experiences pain.

4. Let go of anger and resentment: Holding onto anger and resentment towards others can prevent you from being compassionate and forgiving. It's important to acknowledge and process your feelings, but also to let them go and move forward.

5. Practice forgiveness: Forgiveness is a choice to let go of anger and resentment towards someone who has hurt you. It doesn't mean that you condone their behaviour or forget what happened, but it does mean that you are no longer allowing the hurt to control your life. Forgiveness can be a difficult and ongoing process, but it can also be incredibly liberating and healing.

Remember that cultivating compassion and forgiveness is a process that takes time and effort. Be patient and kind with yourself and others, keep practicing.

The transformative power of forgiveness

Forgiveness is a powerful tool that can transform individuals and communities. When someone forgives, they let go of anger, resentment, and the desire for revenge, and instead choose to show empathy and compassion towards the person who has wronged them. Forgiveness allows individuals to move past negative experiences and emotions and can lead to healing and a sense of peace.

Forgiveness can also have a transformative effect on relationships. When both parties are willing to forgive and move forward, it can lead to a deeper understanding, trust, and appreciation for each other. In some cases, forgiveness can even lead to reconciliation and renewed closeness.

Forgiveness is not always easy, and it does not mean that the offender's actions are excused or forgotten. However, the act of forgiving can be a powerful tool for personal growth and healing. By forgiving, individuals can release themselves from the burden of anger and resentment and move towards a more positive and fulfilling future.

Chapter 7: Letting Go of Control

Understanding the illusion of control

The illusion of control is a cognitive bias that refers to our tendency to overestimate our ability to control events or outcomes that are determined by chance or outside factors. This bias can lead us to believe that we have more control over a situation than we actually do and can cause us to engage in behaviours or make decisions that are not rational or beneficial.

The illusion of control is often seen in situations where chance or luck plays a role, such as gambling or investing. For example, a person may believe that they have a higher chance of winning a game of chance if they have some kind of control over the outcome, such as by choosing their own numbers or using a certain strategy. Similarly, investors may believe that they can control the stock market by making certain trades or following certain patterns.

However, chance, and outside factors often play a much larger role in these situations than we realize. While we may have some control over our actions and decisions, the outcomes are often determined by factors beyond our control, such as luck, market conditions, or the actions of others.

Understanding the illusion of control is important because it can help us make more rational and realistic decisions. By recognizing that we may not have as much control over a situation as we think we do, we can avoid making decisions based on false assumptions or beliefs, and instead focus on factors that we can control.

The benefits of letting go of control.

Letting go of control can have several benefits, including:

1. Reduced stress and anxiety: When we try to control everything, we often become overwhelmed and stressed. Letting go of control can help us relax and reduce anxiety.

2. Increased creativity: When we let go of control, we open ourselves up to new possibilities and ideas. This can lead to increased creativity and innovation.

3. Improved relationships: When we try to control others, it can strain our relationships. Letting go of control can lead to more harmonious relationships and better communication.

4. Greater flexibility: Letting go of control can help us be more adaptable to change and more flexible in our thinking.

5. Increased trust: Letting go of control can help us build trust in ourselves and in others. When we trust that things will work out, we can let go of the need to control everything.

Overall, letting go of control can lead to greater peace of mind, improved relationships, and increased creativity and flexibility.

Techniques for releasing the need for control.

Releasing the need for control can be a difficult task, as it often stems from a deep-seated fear or anxiety. However, there are several techniques that can help individuals let go of the need for control:

1. Mindfulness: Practicing mindfulness can help individuals become more aware of their thoughts and feelings and learn to observe them without judgment. This can help reduce the need for control and increase acceptance of uncertainty.

2. Letting go of perfectionism: Perfectionism often leads to a need for control, as individuals strive to create the perfect outcome. However, letting go of perfectionism can help individuals embrace imperfection and learn to let go of control.

3. Embracing uncertainty: Accepting that there are many things in life that are beyond our control can help individuals let go of the need for control.

Embracing uncertainty can also help individuals develop resilience and adaptability.

4. Identifying triggers: Understanding what triggers the need for control can help individuals learn to recognize when they are feeling anxious or fearful and develop coping mechanisms to manage these feelings.

5. Seeking support: Talking to a therapist or a trusted friend can help individuals process their feelings and develop strategies for letting go of the need for control.

6. Taking small steps: Trying new things and taking small risks can help individuals build confidence and reduce the need for control. This can help individuals learn to trust themselves and others and embrace the unknown.

Chapter 8: Finding Meaning and Purpose

How to find meaning and purpose in difficult situations

Finding meaning and purpose in difficult situations can be a challenging but important process for personal growth and resilience. Here are some strategies that may help:

1. Reframe the situation: Try to view the situation from a different perspective. Ask yourself, "What can I learn from this experience?" or "How can I grow from this?"

2. Find meaning in the struggle: Look for ways in which the difficulty you are facing may help you become a better, stronger person in the long run. Consider how you can use this experience to help others who may face similar struggles.

3. Focus on what you can control: Identify what aspects of the situation you have control over and focus on acting in those areas. This can help you feel more empowered and less helpless.

4. Practice gratitude: Even in difficult situations, there are often things to be grateful for. Take some time to reflect on the positive aspects of your life and express gratitude for them.

5. Seek support: Don't be afraid to reach out to others for support. Talking to a trusted friend, family member, or mental health professional can help you process your feelings and gain perspective on the situation.

Remember, finding meaning and purpose in difficult situations takes time and effort, and it's okay to struggle with it. Be patient with yourself and keep working towards a positive outlook.

 The connection between non-resistance and finding meaning.

Non-resistance, or the practice of accepting things as they are without attempting to change them, can be related to finding meaning in a few ways.

First, when we resist things that we cannot change, we can experience negative emotions like frustration, anger, and anxiety. By practicing non-resistance, we can avoid these negative emotions and instead focus on accepting the present moment as it is. This can help us find peace and contentment during difficult circumstances.

Second, non-resistance can help us cultivate a sense of meaning and purpose in life. When we resist reality, we may become caught up in our own desires and expectations, which can lead to feelings of dissatisfaction and emptiness. By accepting what is, we can focus on what truly matters to us and find meaning in our experiences.

Finally, non-resistance can help us develop a sense of compassion and connection with others. When we resist reality, we may become isolated and disconnected from those around us. By accepting what is, we can open ourselves up to the experiences of others and develop a greater sense of empathy and understanding. This can help us find deeper meaning in our relationships and interactions with others.

Techniques for discovering our life's purpose.

Discovering one's life purpose can be a challenging and ongoing process, and there is no one-size-fits-all approach to achieving it. However, here are some techniques that may help:

1. Reflect on your values: Start by examining your core values and what you believe is important in life. What motivates you? What causes do you care about? What are the things that you would be willing to sacrifice for?

2. Explore your passions: Consider the activities that bring you joy and fulfilment. What are the things that you enjoy doing, even if they don't necessarily feel like "work"? What topics or subjects do you find yourself constantly gravitating towards?

3. Identify your strengths: Think about the things that you excel at and the skills that come naturally to you. What do you do well? What do others

often ask for your help with? These strengths may be clues to your life's purpose.

4. Pay attention to your intuition: Sometimes, our intuition can guide us towards our life's purpose. Pay attention to the thoughts and feelings that arise when you're considering different options or paths. Listen to your inner voice.

5. Experiment with different experiences: Sometimes, we may not discover our life's purpose until we've tried a variety of experiences. Take the time to explore different career paths, hobbies, and interests. Each experience may offer valuable insights and help you understand what you truly want in life.

6. Seek guidance: Consider talking to a mentor, coach, or counsellor who can offer guidance and support as you explore your life's purpose. They may be able to offer new perspectives and help you identify blind spots.

Remember, discovering your life's purpose is a journey that may take time and effort. Be patient and kind to yourself as you explore and experiment with different possibilities.

Chapter 9: Embracing Change

The inevitability of change in life

Change is a fundamental aspect of life that is inevitable and constant. Everything around us is in a constant state of flux, and our lives are no exception. Whether it is change in our relationships, careers, health, or personal circumstances, change is an essential part of our growth and development.

The inevitability of change can be both exciting and challenging. On the one hand, change can bring new opportunities, experiences, and perspectives that enrich our lives and help us to grow as individuals. On the other hand, change can also be difficult and stressful, especially when it disrupts the stability and comfort of our routines and familiar environments.

However, it's essential to recognize that change is necessary for personal growth and development. Without change, we would remain stagnant and unable to adapt to new situations and challenges. Embracing change and learning to navigate its ups and downs is an essential skill that can help us to become more resilient, flexible, and adaptable individuals.

Ultimately, the inevitability of change is a reminder that life is a journey full of twists and turns. By embracing change and learning to navigate its challenges, we can make the most of our experiences and continue to grow and develop as individuals.

How to embrace change without resistance

Embracing change can be difficult, especially when we are comfortable with the status quo or when we have invested a lot of time and effort in a particular way of doing things. However, there are several ways to embrace change without resistance:

1. Understand the reason for the change: When we understand the reason for the change, it can be easier to accept it. Take the time to understand why the change is happening and how it will benefit you or the organization.

2. Keep an open mind: Try to approach the change with an open mind. Avoid making assumptions or jumping to conclusions before you have all the facts.

3. Focus on the positive: Instead of dwelling on the negatives, focus on the positives that the change may bring. Think about new opportunities, skills you may learn, or ways that the change may improve your life or work.

4. Stay flexible: Be willing to adapt to new situations and be open to new ideas. Don't be afraid to experiment and try new approaches.

5. Act: Instead of waiting for the change to happen to you, act and be proactive. Look for ways to get involved in the change process and take ownership of your role in making the change successful.

6. Seek support: Change can be difficult, and it's important to seek support from others. Talk to friends, colleagues, or a mentor to help you navigate the change and provide support and encouragement.

Remember, change is a natural part of life, and it can bring new opportunities and growth. By embracing change with an open mind and a positive attitude, you can adapt and thrive in a changing world.

Techniques for adapting to change.

Adapting to change can be challenging, but there are several techniques that can be helpful in navigating the process:

1. Maintain a positive attitude: A positive attitude can help you approach change with an open mind and a willingness to learn and grow.

2. Be flexible: Being flexible allows you to adjust to new situations and adapt to changing circumstances. Try to remain open to new ideas and ways of doing things.

3. Stay informed: Keeping up to date with information about the change can help you understand why it is happening and what you can do to adapt.

4. Seek support: It can be helpful to seek support from friends, family, or colleagues during times of change. Talking to someone who has been through a similar experience can provide reassurance and guidance.

5. Focus on what you can control: While some changes may be beyond your control, there are often things you can control. Focus on what you can do to make the best of the situation.

6. Take care of yourself: Change can be stressful, so it's important to take care of yourself both physically and mentally. Eat healthily, get enough sleep, and engage in activities that help you relax and reduce stress.

7. Embrace the opportunity: Change can bring new opportunities for growth and development. Try to approach the change as an opportunity to learn new skills and expand your knowledge.

Chapter 10: Living a Non-Resistant Life

Integrating the principles of non-resistance into daily life

The principles of non-resistance are often associated with Eastern spiritual traditions such as Taoism and Buddhism and can be applied to daily life in a variety of ways. Here are some suggestions:

1. Let go of expectations: Non-resistance involves accepting things as they are, without trying to force them to be different. This means letting go of expectations and embracing whatever comes your way. Practice being open to new experiences and detaching from specific outcomes.

2. Practice mindfulness: This involves being fully present in the moment and observing your thoughts and emotions without judgment. Mindfulness can help you become more aware of your resistance to certain experiences or situations and learn to let go of them.

3. Focus on the positive: Non-resistance involves focusing on the positive aspects of a situation or experience, rather than dwelling on the negative. This can help you stay in a more positive, open-minded state of mind and attract more positive experiences into your life.

4. Cultivate compassion: Non-resistance involves being compassionate towards yourself and others. When you encounter difficult situations or people, try to approach them with kindness and understanding, rather than resistance or judgment.

5. Embrace change: Non-resistance involves accepting that change is inevitable and embracing it as an opportunity for growth and learning. Practice being open to new experiences and learning from them, rather than resisting them out of fear or discomfort.

Remember that non-resistance is a practice, and it takes time and effort to integrate these principles into your daily life. Be patient with yourself and keep practicing, and over time you may find that you are able to approach life with more ease and grace.

How to sustain a non-resistant mind-set

Sustaining a non-resistant mind-set can be challenging, but it is possible with consistent practice and awareness. Here are some tips to help you cultivate and maintain a non-resistant mind-set:

1. Practice mindfulness: Mindfulness involves paying attention to the present moment without judgment. Regular mindfulness practice can help you become more aware of your thoughts and emotions and learn to observe them without reacting.

2. Accept what is: Accepting what is means acknowledging the reality of your situation without resistance or denial. It doesn't mean that you have to like what is happening, but rather that you are willing to face it head-on.

3. Let go of control: Trying to control everything can create resistance and stress. Instead, focus on what you can control and let go of the rest. This means trusting the process and having faith that things will work out as they are meant to.

4. Practice gratitude: Gratitude is a powerful tool for cultivating a non-resistant mind-set. Take time each day to reflect on what you are grateful for. This can help shift your focus from what you don't have to what you do have.

5. Cultivate compassion: Compassion involves treating yourself and others with kindness and understanding. When you approach life with compassion, you are less likely to resist what is happening and more likely to find solutions and opportunities for growth.

Remember that sustaining a non-resistant mind-set is an ongoing process. It requires consistent practice and patience with yourself. Don't be discouraged if you slip up or encounter challenges along the way. With time and effort, you can develop a non-resistant mind-set that will serve you well in all areas of your life.

Epilogue

As life continues, we will inevitably face challenges and difficulties that can feel overwhelming. But rather than struggling against these storms, we can learn to find peace by embracing non-resistance.
When we resist the challenges that come our way, we only amplify our suffering. We may feel frustrated, angry, or resentful towards the situation, and we may feel powerless to change it. But when we learn to let go of resistance and accept what is, we can find a sense of calm even during chaos.
This doesn't mean that we should simply give up or stop working towards our goals. Rather, it means that we should approach challenges with a sense of openness and flexibility and be willing to adapt and adjust our plans as needed. By doing so, we can cultivate a sense of resilience that allows us to weather the storms of life with greater ease and grace.
As we learn to embrace non-resistance, we may also find that our perspective shifts. We may begin to see challenges as opportunities for growth and learning, rather than as obstacles to be overcome. We may find that we are better able to connect with others and to appreciate the beauty and richness of life, even in difficult times.
Ultimately, finding peace in the storm requires a willingness to let go of control and to trust in the unfolding of life. It requires a willingness to be present in each moment, and to cultivate a sense of gratitude for all that we have. By doing so, we can find a deep sense of peace and fulfilment, even amidst life's greatest challenges.